WHY UNIVERSE?

NIHAL MUDGAL

DEDICATED TO YOU...

May the Universe bring you love and joy for your entire existence.

That is my intention for you

and for the world.

Contents

Contents

Message From The Author

Before You Read, I Want You To Know That You Are Very Lucky And Blessesd By The Universe So You Can Get This Precious Knowledge. And You Are Under This 1% Because You Try Effort, Investing Your Money In Knowlege Rather Buying Fake Fancy Stuff.

I'm Very Thankful For The Universe For Giving Me Chance To Give Impact On Many Souls.

I Want You To Know That **This Is Very Short Book;** There Are Not Many Sentences, Difficult Fancy Words I Wrote This Book As Concisely As Possible Because I Want To Foster A Community Of Highly Ambitious Individuals And Teach Them About Manifestation. This Is A Beginner's Guide For Those Who May Not Know Much About The Topic.

My Intention For Keeping The Book Short Is To Instill A Sense Of Achievement. Whenever You Finish Reading A Book, There's A Rush Of Dopamine In Your Brain. I Want All My Readers To Experience This Feeling, Empowering Them To Believe They Can Achieve Anything In Their Lives.

As A Famous Quote States, "little By Little Is Better Than Nothing At All.

Because Before I Also Don't like Reading Books that much. I Want My Solution To Be One Line, One Word. So In This Book I'm Sharing Just A Sentences Scientific Solutions, Techinques And Excercises Of How Manifestation Works? What Is Manifestation? So You Don't Feel Bored With This Book **You Can Finish In Less Than 2 Weeks.**

I Want Everyone To Be See Everyone Happy In Thier Lives, Getting To Achieve What They Want, What You Wish, And What They Always Prayed For.

All The Best, Happy Reading.

SHRI RADHA!

Acknowledgements

I bow to Your divine presence my beloved **Lord Shri Hari** , and offer my heartfelt gratitude for the blessings and inspiration that have flowed through me. This book is a humble offering to You, a token of my love and devotion. May it be a source of joy, wisdom, and spiritual growth to all who read it, and may Your divine presence be felt on every page."

"I would like to extend my deepest gratitude to everyone who has supported me on this incredible journey. To My Guru SHRI ANIRUDHACHARYA JI, SHRI PREMANAND JI MAHARAJ, My Mentor SHREYAS MUKATI SIR, My Parents ANJALI MUDGAL & GAGAN MUDGAL and All My loved ones, thank you for your unwavering encouragement, patience, and love. Your presence in my life has been a constant source of inspiration and motivation.

To my **Readers**, thank you for embracing my work and allowing me to share my thoughts, ideas, and passions with you. Your support means the world to me.

And to the **Universe**, thank you for the infinite opportunities, experiences, and lessons that have shaped me into the person I am today. I am humbled and grateful for this incredible journey.

As I sit here, reflecting on the past year, I'm overwhelmed with emotions. For me 2024 was supposed to be a year of growth, success, and happiness, failures, sleepless nights, major downfalls, healing, self-discovery and most important precious lifetime lessons i learnt this year.

My name is **NIHAL MUDGAL.**

I lost myself, only to find my true self. How I hit rock bottom, only to rise again, stronger and wiser.

This year, I faced challenges that shook my confidence, tested my faith, and pushed me to the brink of giving up. Depression crept in, casting a shadow over my life. But amildst the darkness, I found solace in my spiritual journey with **Lord Dwarkadhish**.

Through tears, prayers, and meditation, I began to heal. I discovered the power of manifestation, self-belief, and the unconditional love of the universe. Slowly, I rebuilt my confidence, my sense of purpose, and my connection with myself.

This book is my testament to the human spirit's capacity for resilience. It's a story of hope, faith, and the transformative power of adversity.

Remember that there's a lesson in every challenge, a lesson in every failure, which means your failure don't have to be failures at all; they are just twists in your path to greatness. Join me on this emotional journey, as I share some of my secret manifestation techniqus, healing methods and exercises I learned along the way.

Preface

Welcome to **'WHY UNIVERSE?'**, a journey of self-discovery, spiritual growth, and transformation. As you embark on this path, I invite you to ask yourself a profound question: 'What if the universe had a plan for me, and I had the power to manifest it?'

For centuries, the mysteries of the universe have fascinated and intrigued us. We've searched for answers in the stars, in ancient texts, and in the depths of our own souls. And yet, the most profound truth remains: that we have the power to shape our reality, to manifest our desires, and to create the life we've always dreamed of.

In the following pages, we'll explore the methods and steps of manifestation, a powerful process that has transformed my life and the lives of countless others. We'll delve into the mysteries of the universe, exploring the interconnectedness of all things and the infinite possibilities that lie within us.

Through practical exercises, and spiritual insights, we'll uncover the secrets of manifestation and provide you with the tools and inspiration you need to create the life you desire.

So, I invite you to join me on this journey of discovery, to ask yourself the profound questions, and to unlock the secrets of the universe. Together, let's manifest our dreams, realize our potential, and create a life that is truly extraordinary.

Get ready to unlock the power of manifestation and transform your life forever!

Foreword

As I reflect on the journey that has brought us to this moment, I am reminded of the profound impact that a single question can have on our lives. **'WHY UNIVERSE?'** is more than just a query - it's an invitation to explore the deepest mysteries of existence, to challenge our assumptions, and to discover the infinite possibilities that lie within us.

Nihal Mudgal's book is a testament to the human spirit's capacity for curiosity, resilience, and transformation. Through his personal story, insights, and practical wisdom, Nihal offers us a powerful reminder that we all have the power to shape our reality, to overcome obstacles, and to create the life we desire.

As you embark on this journey with Nihal, I invite you to approach these pages with an open heart, a curious mind, and a willingness to explore the unknown. For in the words of the great poet Rumi, 'What you seek is seeking you."

"THE MIND ACT LIKE AN ENEMY FOR THOSE WHO DON'T CONTROL IT."

~bhagwat gita [5TH CENTURY]

Introduction To Manifestation

The sky was colored violet and gold as the sun dipped below the horizon, casting long shadows on the ground. In the quiet of twilight, in the silence that filled the emptiness, a question echoed in the mind of the Seeker—a question older than eternity itself: **What if I could create my own reality?**

This was not only a thought, but a whisper from the Universe, a calling from deep in the soul. Something deeper stirred—an ancient truth to be remembered.

We've all had those moments when the universe appears to be conspiratorially aligned. You speak a name, and they call. You pray for a door to open, and there's an opening. Initially, we call it coincidence. Yet, as they become more frequent and more loud, another explanation begins to make itself heard: What if I'm not a passive receiver of this existence, but an active participant in its creation?

This is where the manifestation process begins.

The Forgotten Power Within

Since we're born, we are taught that things "happen" to us. We're taught to take the world as something fixed—unchangeable and beyond our control. But the truth is that the power to create reality slumbers in each of us. It's not fantasy. It's not magic. It's the most fundamental law of life: **we attract what we believe, feel, and expect.**

Manifestation is the art of transforming thought into form, imagination into experience, and desire into destiny. It's the language of co-creation between the self

and the Universe.

It is not wishing in the dark, however. It's about putting your thoughts, feelings, energy, and action into alignment with your highest goals. It's about shifting your world within to allow your world outside to come naturally.

Science Meets the Soul

What was mystical is now supported by science. **Quantum physics teaches us that everything in the universe is made up of energy, vibrating at different frequencies. Thoughts, emotions, and beliefs are not mere ethereal whispers in the mind—they are energetic impulses radiating out into the field of possibility.**

The Law of Attraction, rooted in both ancient wisdom and modern psychology, demonstrates that *like attracts like.* If you tune into abundance, love, peace, or success, you draw experiences to you that vibrate at that frequency.

Neuroscience also offers profound confirmation. Through the process of neuroplasticity, the brain is able to rewire itself based on patterns of thought and emotional habits. That is, when you change your mind, you literally change your life.

Manifestation, then, is where science and spirituality intersect. **It is the gateway between what is and what can be.**

Why It Matters

This chapter is not here to convince you, but to awaken you.

Because deep inside, you already know this truth. You've felt it in moments of synchronicity. You've sensed it in your dreams. You've enjoyed it in fleeting moments when everything just "clicked."

Manifestation isn't about controlling the Universe—it's about dancing with it. It's not about ego—it's about alignment. It's not about greed—it's about purpose, clarity, and being the fullest version of your soul's potential.

When you create, you're not just making things better. You're remembering who you are.

The Beginning of the Journey

This book is not just a guide. It is an invitation.

An invitation to learn the divine principles that govern the Universe. An invitation to heal the wounds that keep you stuck in limitation. An invitation to awaken, reclaim your power, and consciously create a life that reflects your highest self.

Whether you're struggling, seeking, or just curious, the manifestation path will change everything—you because it changes you.

So take a breath. Let go of doubt, if only for a moment. And leave your heart open to the truth that the Universe is not something external to you, but in you—reacting to every thought, every feeling, and every intention.

You didn't come here accidentally. You were brought to this moment. The question now is: Are you willing to

remember your power and enter into the life you came to live?

The Universe is waiting.

And your journey starts now.

CHAPTER ONE

UNDERSTANDING MANIFESTATION

It began with a quiet morning. The Seeker sat by the window, watching sunlight spill over the trees. A breeze passed through, carrying the scent of earth and something more subtle—something that couldn't be named, only felt.

As the mind quieted, a question surfaced: I've heard of manifestation... but what does it truly mean? How does it work?

The idea resonated, yet it seemed abstract. **Was it really possible that thoughts construct reality? Was adream created through imagining?** The Seeker read the tales, heard the testimonials, saw the miracles. Yet within, an urge was created—not for belief, but comprehension.

"EVERYHING YOU CAN IMAGINE IS REAL" -PICASO

Beyond Wishful Thinking

Manifestation isn't simply about thinking positive thoughts and waiting for the Universe to deliver. That's a misunderstanding many carry. The truth is more profound—and more personal.

At its core, *manifestation is the process of consciously creating your reality by aligning your thoughts, emotions, beliefs, and actions with your desired outcome. It's not a shortcut to escape life's challenges—it's a tool to meet them with grace, intention, and power.*

When we manifest, **we're not telling the Universe what to do; we're working with it.**

The Mechanics of Manifestation

To grasp manifestation, think of the Universe as a big energy field full of infinite possibilities, vibrating with every potential out there. Quantum physics calls this the quantum field—a place where everything exists in a state of potential until measured or affected by consciousness.

You are not outside of this domain. You are a living, breathing manifestation of it.

Your thoughts are electrical currents. Your feelings are magnetic waves. Together, they create a vibration—a energetic frequency that engages the Universe. This vibration communicates a message: This is who I am. This is what I believe. This is what I expect.

And the Universe answers.

This is not superstition. It's resonance. As tuning forks will resonate with each other when they have the same frequency, your inner reality draws outer experiences that reflect it.

When your mind is clear, your heart is open, and your beliefs are congruent, you enter coherence—a field of energy harmony that sculpts reality with accuracy.

The Subconscious Role

The Seeker found that manifestation does not start with desires, but with beliefs—particularly those lying hidden in the subconscious.

The subconscious mind holds all of our early programming: worthiness, love, success, and possibility beliefs. These scripts frequently operate below awareness, shaping our choices, expectations, and boundaries in silence.

If you become aware that you want abundance but unconsciously feel that you aren't worthy of it, your vibration is conflicted. The message to the Universe is confused. And thus, the outcome mirrors that inner conflict.

Manifestation means knowing yourself.

It involves becoming conscious of the beliefs that clog your flow. It involves healing the emotional wounds that warp your frequency. It involves choosing alignment over fear, time and time again.

Manifestation and Emotions

Feelings are not only responses—they're energetic signals. Every feeling has a frequency: joy, love, gratitude, and peace are high-frequency emotions that attract experiences of abundance and flow. Fear, guilt, anger, and doubt produce a denser vibration, tending to attract struggle or stagnation.

The Seeker started to understand: **manifestation is not simply about thinking—it's about feeling. It's about feeling the emotion of the result prior to it manifesting.** When you feel the joy, love, or success in the now moment, you turn on the vibration that brings it into form.

This is why **gratitude** is such a potent manifesting force. When you are grateful, you are saying: I already have. I already am. And the Universe mirrors that belief back to you.

The Final Bridge

But even this is not the whole story.

Manifestation involves action—not desperate striving, but inspired movement. When you're in alignment of thought, feeling, and belief, the Universe opens doors. But it is you who must walk through them.

The Seeker recalled a truth reverberated throughout ages past: **Faith without works is dead.**

You have to be there. You have to make the call. Send the email. Accept the offer. Let go of the past. Start the project. Trust the vision.

Action is the bridge between the invisible and the visible.

Manifestation Is a Way of Living

Manifestation isn't something you do once. It's a way of being.

It's being aware of your power. It's being responsible for your energy. It's tuning yourself to possibility, even when the world resists.

It's healing, growing, aligning—again and again.

As the Seeker observed the sun rise higher in the sky, a peaceful certainty took hold. Manifestation wasn't some mystical idea. It was real. It was inside. It was working all along, whether consciously or unconsciously.

The secret was this: to become aware of what you're creating each moment, and to select it with deliberation, lucidity, and love.

And in awareness, the Seeker smiled.

Because now, they knew.

The Law of Attraction

It was evening when the Seeker stood alone under a star-filled sky, every star shining like a faraway dream that would soon come true. The night's silence wasn't hollow-it was alive. And somewhere in that great quietude, the truth lay in wait to be heard.

The Seeker's eyes closed and they whispered: If manifestation exists, what force binds my thoughts to the universe? What invisible string draws desire into being? The response came like a soothing wave—**The Law of Attraction.**

The Universe's Magnetic Law

The Law of Attraction is among the most potent universal laws. Simply stated: **like attracts like.** Whatever **you give attention to—intentionally or involuntarily—you attract to yourself.**

If your mind is centered in love, joy, and abundance, you will draw experiences that are in accord with those frequencies. And if your mind is filled with fear, doubt, and lack, the same will work.

The Seeker had always thought life was arbitrary, that blessings fell to the fortunate and pain to the unfortunate. But with this law, everything changed. It showed that life doesn't answer to what you desire—it answers to what you're being.

The Law of Attraction never stops, whether you think it does or not. It doesn't discriminate, it doesn't pick and choose—it simply reacts to the energetic vibration you put out.

Thoughts Become Things

Within the quiet of their practice, the Seeker started to notice something remarkable: thoughts are not quiet. They are messages. Every one vibrates at a specific frequency and transmits a message out into the quantum field.

When you repeat a thought in your mind—particularly one that has an emotional charge—it becomes magnetic. It starts to influence the reality you perceive, first quietly, then inexorably.

"One positive thought can become a belief. A belief can turn into a habit. And a habit becomes a life."

The Law of Attraction, therefore, isn't about daydreaming—it's about deliberately focusing your thoughts, emotions, and beliefs on the life you decide to build.

Emotion: The Fuel of Attraction

The Seeker discovered another reality: *emotion is the driver of attraction.*

Your emotions are not just responses to life—they are energetic vibrations that either expand or contract your magnetic field. **When you experience happiness, love, appreciation, or enthusiasm, your vibration increases. When you experience fear, worry, or self-doubt, it diminishes.**

So when you're imagining your ideal life, it's not just a matter of visualizing it—you have to feel it. You have to feel the freedom, the peace, the abundance like it already is. Because in the energetic universe, it is.

Emotion takes intention and turns it into vibration. And **vibration is the language the Universe speaks.**

Belief Shapes Reality

The Seeker asked: **What if I have positive thinking but I still attract negativity?**

The solution was deeper than thought—within belief.

The Law of Attraction responds to the inner beliefs based in your subconscious mind, not the surface-level desires. You might proclaim, "I deserve love," but if your inner belief mutters, "I'm not enough," the Universe will react to the vibration of your inner voice.

This is the reason why healing is necessary. You need to discover and reprogram the inner beliefs that negate your desires. Only then will your frequency get clear, coherent, and potent.

Visualization and Alignment

The Seeker visualized each day—shutting their eyes, stepping into the life they wanted, experiencing the feeling of it as if it actually existed. And gradually, something did change. Possibilities emerged. New individuals came into their life. Situations shifted without rational explanation.

Because visualization, when merged with belief and emotion, is a strong magnetic force.

But the Seeker also discovered that the Law of Attraction isn't about getting—it's about becoming. It's not about acquiring something external to you. It's about getting into alignment so thoroughly with your intended reality that it becomes who you are.

You don't attract money—you become money. You don't find love—you are love. You don't wish for peace—you are peace.

The Universe Responds to Clarity

Clarity is a superpower. The Universe cannot bring you what you are unclear about. The Seeker learned this after numerous failed attempts to manifest dreams that were unclear, half-hearted, or fear-tainted.

When your desire is clear, your intention clear, and your belief firm, the Law of Attraction starts working with clarity and speed.

Write it. Feel it. Say it. Believe it.

Inspired Action and Surrender

But there is one last key: **action.**

Manifestation with the Law of Attraction is not passive. The Universe opens doors, but you walk through them. When you get a nudge, take it. When an idea stirs you, do something about it. When life encourages you to move forward, say yes.

And once you've done your share, let go. Trust. Release how and when. The Seeker discovered that obsession stunts the flow. Surrender, by contrast, opens wide.

The Law of Attraction doesn't take effort—it takes alignment. And once you're in alignment, life starts to respond in ways that feel magical, yet normal.

Living the Law

Now, when the Seeker steps under the stars, they no longer sense apart from them. They know they are composed of the same energy, communicating the same language, dancing in the same field of creation.

The Law of Attraction isn't merely a spiritual principle—it's a lifestyle. A way of thinking, feeling, choosing, and trusting.

And the most gorgeous part?

You've been using it all along. Now, you get to use it consciously.

"The universe will send you exactly what you ask for and then it will send you a distraction to see if you were really ready to receive what you wanted." - *NIHAL MUDGAL*

The Power of Belief

There was one point when the Seeker were standing at the precipice of a path which they had not traversed No map, no directions—just an inward whisper, You can. And then there was the louder one proclaiming, You've previously failed. You're not yet ready. You're not yet sufficient.

And that was when the Seeker understood: the biggest fight isn't between success and failure, light and darkness, or even want and terror. It is waged quietly, between faith and doubt.

The way we live our lives is not set by fate or coincidence alone. **It is etched by belief.**

What Is a Belief?

A belief isn't just a thought. It's a habit. A filter. An instruction.

A belief is a thought repeated so many times—particularly in emotionally charged situations—that it becomes a truth in the subconscious mind. And helpful or harmful, your beliefs create your reality.

They are the architects of your actions, the guardians of your potential, and the invisible gatekeepers of what

you do or do not let into your life.

The Seeker learned this reality in the quiet of reflection: You don't receive what you want, you receive what you feel you deserve.

How Beliefs Are Created

The Seeker followed their beliefs back to childhood—where voices of authority told them what was possible. *"You'll never succeed." "Money doesn't grow on trees." "You must suffer to be spiritual."*

These words, said enough times, became imprints on the subconscious. And those imprints silently ruled the Seeker's life.

Beliefs are usually inherited—not only from parents or culture, but from centuries of collective fear, lack, and unworthiness. Most people never challenge these internal programs. They live in them, not even realizing they're there.

But here's the miracle: *beliefs can be altered.*

Science of Belief: Rewiring the Mind

The Seeker's question led them into the science of the mind. Neuroscience taught them a deep truth—through neuroplasticity, the brain is not set. It is moldable, ever-changing, ever-rewiring itself on the basis of repetition, emotion, and experience.

Each time you state a new empowering belief, you build new neural pathways. With repetition and emotional energy enough, those pathways get stronger, and old limiting beliefs start to weaken and break down.

You can actually rewire your brain for success, prosperity, peace, or love. Not by force—but through conscious repetition and trust.

Belief Creates Experience

Someone who feels that they are not deserving of love will destroy every relationship, even when love is freely given. Someone who feels that they cannot succeed will miss opportunities right in front of them.

Not because the way things really are is cruel, but because belief screens out perception.

Your beliefs become self-fulfilling prophecies. They determine how you see the world, and what you permit yourself to see, receive, or reject.

That's why **belief is the foundation of manifestation. You can visualize, affirm, and want—but if your belief system dictates, "This isn't possible for me," then that belief becomes your truth.**

The Universe doesn't react to your thoughts. It reacts to your certainty.

Healing Limiting Beliefs

The Seeker knew they needed to challenge the beliefs that no longer served them. And so, they asked:

What do I believe about myself?

What do I believe about love, success, and abundance?

Who taught me those beliefs were true?

Are they empowering—or holding me back?

This was the start of inner healing.

Limiting beliefs lose their power when they are brought into awareness. Once revealed, they can be rewritten—gently, patiently, on purpose.

The Seeker used daily affirmations, visualizations, mirror work, and emotional release. Every step rewired a part of their inner world. Over time, the inner voice changed—from doubt to trust, from fear to courage.

And with the changing beliefs, so did their reality.

Empowered Beliefs That Change Lives

Truth- and soul-power-based beliefs are the source of miracles.

I am worthy of love, joy, and abundance.

I am the author of my life.

The Universe is on my side.

All is working for my highest good.

My past does not determine my future.

I trust in my dreams, and I trust the timing.

These are not affirmations—they are keys that open a new level of existence.

When the Seeker started living out of these convictions, they sensed the difference. Individuals treated them differently. Opportunities streamed. Synchronicities grew. Not because the world had altered, but because they had.

You Become What You Believe

Finally, the Seeker again stood on that strange road. But this time, the inner voice spoke:

You can.
You are ready.
You were born for this.

And that faith was enough to make the first step—and the second—and the third.

Because when you have faith in your vision, the Universe starts to organize itself according to your belief. Doors open. Assistance comes. And the impossible starts to become reality.

Belief is your doorway.
Not only to manifestation—but to healing, transformation, and boundless creation.
Alter your beliefs, and you alter your world.

"WHEN EVERTHING IS BREAKING DOWN, AND YOU DO THE THE RIGHT THING, EVERYTHING BUILDS BACK UP FASTER [AND GREATER] THAN YOU'VE EVER IMAGINED." -NIHAL MUDGAL

Set clear intention

The Seeker once sat in the stillness of the woods, observing leaves twirl in the breeze. The world was alive—moving, breathing, reacting. But within, they felt lost, as if life progressed while they stood still.

They had studied manifestation, belief, and the Law of Attraction. But still, their journey seemed disjointed. Progress seemed fuzzy.

That's when a question resonated within:
What do I really want?

And then, in a flash of epiphany, the response came not in word, but revelation: **Clarity is power.**

Why Intention Matters

An intention is not just a wish. An intention is not just a goal.
An intention is a voluntary command to the Universe.

It asserts: This is what I am deciding. This is what I'm aligning. This is who I am becoming.

The Seeker understood that they had been wanting change for years without ever naming it. Their visions were fuzzy—like smoke. But the Universe does not answer to smoke. It answers to fire. And intention is the ignition that ignites that fire.

Just as a vessel requires coordinates to arrive at its destination, your mind, energy, and actions need the anchor of clear intention to proceed in sync.

The Energy Behind Intention

Intentions are not simply mental choices. Intentions have energy.

When you purposefully intend from your heart, your whole self starts lining up. The cells of your physical body pay attention. Your subconscious mind is activated. Your emotions become powered. The Universe receives your frequency and reflects it back to you.

An intention creates a ripple in the quantum field. The ripple starts to attract circumstances, people, and situations that vibrate with what you've chosen.

But when intentions are unclear, the energy is scattered—and so are the results.

The Seeker learned: an unclear mind sends a confused signal. But a focused intention sends a powerful vibration.

Intention vs. Expectation

There's a sacred distinction the Seeker had to learn through experience: **Intention is not expectation**.

Expectation is rigid. It clings to outcomes and timelines. It says, "It must happen like this, or it means I've failed."

But intention is malleable. It flows with trust. It announces, "This is what I prefer, and I trust the Universe to deliver it in the highest manner, at the most opportune time."

Intention gives direction. Surrender brings magic.

How to Set Clear Intentions

The Seeker started to adopt a sacred daily ritual, one that was both simple and profound:

1. Go Within: In meditation or silence, ask yourself—What do I really want? What feels in alignment with my soul?

2. Get Specific: Wishes that are vague create vague outcomes. Instead of "I want abundance," say, "I intend to generate steady income doing what I love."

3. Feel It Fully: When you state your intention, feel it in your body. Visualize how you will feel when it happens.

Emotions intensify energy.

4. Write It Down: Making it concrete. Bringing the intention into the physical world.

5. Repeat with Faith: Return to your intention every day—not with neediness, but with joy and conviction. Make it your new inner truth.

6. Align Your Actions: Allow your decisions, words, and routines to be an expression of your intention. Action is how you demonstrate to the Universe that you're ready.

7. Let Go of the How: Have you faith that the Universe will handle the details. Remain open to routes you did not anticipate.

The Seeker applied this practice every day, and things really did start to change—not always immediately, but always exactly as they should.

New doors opened. Insight appeared. Even challenges started to appear as redirections to the very goal they had established.

Intention Aligns the Mind, Heart, and Spirit

The Seeker learned something greater: *when you place a real intention—not ego, but soul—it changes you.*

You start thinking differently. You speak with more intention. You walk with more awareness. You no longer pursue—because you have become magnetic.

The ultimate power of intention lies not in what it gets you, but in who you become as a result of it.

The Seeker had once drifted through life wondering, Why am I not getting what I want?

Now they walked with serene conviction, proclaiming: This is what I choose to bring into being. And I am prepared for it.

And the Universe replied—**not due to circumstance, but due to clarity.**

**A scattered mind generates scattered energy.
A clear intention generates a clear path.
What you intend, you become. What you become, you attract.**

*"THERE ARE WORSE CRIMES THAN BURNING BOOK.
ONE OF THEM IS NOT READING THEM." -UNKNOWN*

CHAPTER TWO

BASIC MANIFESTATION TECHNIQUES

The Seeker once asked the wise one, "If I know the Law of Attraction… if I believe… and I set intentions… why do my dreams still feel distant?"

The wise one smiled and said,

"Because knowing is not enough. Belief must become practice. Intention must meet action. Energy must be moved."

And so began the Seeker's journey into **the techniques—the sacred tools that bridge thought and form, spirit and matter, imagination and reality.**

Manifestation is not a mysterious power reserved for the few. *It is a skill, a science, a sacred practice anyone can learn. And like any skill, it begins with the basics.*

1. Visualization

See it before it exists.

The Seeker learned that the subconscious mind cannot distinguish between vividly imagined experiences and physical reality. So each day, they closed their eyes and stepped into the future they desired—**as if it were happening now.**

They saw the details. Felt the emotions. Heard the sounds. They imagined the smile on their face when the dream came true.

Why it works:
Visualization activates *the reticular activating system (RAS)* in the brain, helping you notice opportunities aligned with your goal. It also shifts your energetic frequency to match your desired reality.

How to practice:
Sit in stillness for 5–10 minutes daily.
Breathe deeply and calm your mind.
Visualize your desired reality in detail.
Feel it in your heart—joy, gratitude, peace.
End with a smile and a silent thank you.

2. Affirmations

Speak it until it becomes your truth.

The Seeker used to say, "I hope I can." But they learned to say, "I am already becoming."

Affirmations are powerful statements that reprogram the subconscious mind. Spoken with emotion and repetition, they dissolve limiting beliefs and install empowering ones.

Why it works:

Your subconscious is shaped by repeated thought. Affirmations restructure internal narratives and build new neural pathways.

Examples:

I am worthy of success and happiness.

Everything I desire is already on its way to me.

I trust the Universe and surrender to divine timing.

Tips:

Speak in the present tense.

Make it positive and specific.

Repeat with emotion, especially in the morning and before sleep.

3. Gratitude

Feel blessed before the blessing arrives.

The Seeker discovered that the fastest way to shift energy is not to ask—but to give thanks. Gratitude is the vibration of receivership. It says, "I already have. I already am."

Gratitude opens the heart and raises your frequency. When you're grateful, you align with abundance—and abundance flows where it is appreciated.

Daily practice:

Write 5 things you're grateful for every morning.

Include things not yet manifested—as if they've already arrived.

Say: "Thank you, Universe, for my financial freedom, vibrant health, and soulful love."

4. Scripting

Write your reality into existence.

The Seeker began journaling their life—not as it was, but as they desired it to be. They wrote pages like a diary from the future, describing their dreams in the present tense, full of feeling and clarity.

Why it works:
Scripting activates the imagination, emotion, and belief systems—anchoring intentions into the subconscious and aligning energy with outcomes.

How to script:
Set a quiet space. Use a special notebook.
Begin with "I am so happy and grateful now that..."
Describe your life vividly: sights, feelings, people, moments.
Re-read your script often and let the emotion sink in.

5. Acting As If

Become the version of you who already has it.

The Seeker realized the secret wasn't to chase the dream, but to embody the energy of having it now. They began making decisions like the version of them who had already manifested the vision.

Why it works:
"Acting as if" bridges the gap between present reality and future manifestation. It shifts identity, and identity shapes behavior—which shapes outcome.

Example practices:
Dress, speak, and move with confidence.
Make small choices that align with your desired future.

Speak about your vision as a certainty, not a hope.

6. Vision Board

Place your vision where your eyes can see.
The Seeker filled a board with images, quotes, and symbols of their dream life. This visual reminder kept their energy focused and inspired.

Why it works:
Visual cues strengthen focus and keep intention alive. Your brain is highly visual, and consistent exposure helps imprint the vision in the subconscious.

Tips:
Use pictures that evoke emotion and clarity.
Place your board where you'll see it daily.
Look at it with joy and trust, not desperation.

7. Meditation

Align with the field of infinite possibilities.
The Seeker sat in silence each day—not to get, but to align. Through meditation, they released resistance, quieted fear, and returned to the present moment—the only place where true creation begins.

Why it works:
Meditation lowers resistance, calms the nervous system, and deepens connection to the quantum field—where intention, thought, and emotion create reality.

Practice:
Start with 10 minutes a day.

Focus on your breath, a mantra, or the feeling of already having.

Let go of outcome—just be.

You don't need to do all techniques at once. Choose what resonates. Practice daily. Trust the process. The power is not in the ritual—it's in the consistency, the belief, and the emotion behind it.

The Seeker understood, finally:

"Manifestation is not about asking the Universe to give me something I lack. It is about aligning with the truth that everything I desire already exists—and I am worthy of it."

Master the basics. Practice them with love. And soon, what once felt far away will begin arriving—softly, steadily, miraculously.

"LITTLE BY LITTLE IS BETTER THAN NOTHING AT ALL." *-NIHAL MUDGAL*

Visualization

The Seeker used to ascend a still hill in the early dawn. At each step, she breathed her desires into the air—success, love, meaning, serenity. But despite the genuineness of the words, they were hollow, as if the Universe had yet to listen.

At the top, the Seeker encountered an old wise one sitting under a blooming tree. The Seeker questioned, "Why don't my desires get answered even when I truly believe and pray?"

The sage shut their eyes and responded,
"You say what you will. But have you looked at it—really looked at it—with the eyes of your soul?"

The Seeker was silent.
For the first time, they understood: **manifestation is not so much about asking—it is about looking at it prior to its manifestation.**

What Is Visualization?

Visualization is the skill of perceiving with your inner eyes—imagination not as fantasy, but as a blue print for what is possible. It's mentally rehearsing your ideal future in such detailed accuracy that your mind, body, and energy start to accept it as fact.

It is dreaming accurately. Wishing clearly. Believing so intensely that the Universe has no option but to react.

Why Visualization Works

The Seeker discovered that visualization is not mere wishful thinking. It is supported by science, spirit, and the laws of the Universe.

1. Neurological Power:
When you visualize an experience, the brain fires up the same neural pathways as if you were actually living it. This conditions your mind and body for success, focus, and confidence.

2. Subconscious Programming:
Your subconscious mind controls 95% of your behavior. Visualization plants new beliefs and identities in the subconscious, changing your reality from the inside out.

3. Quantum Connection:
In the quantum field, all is potential. When you regularly visualize a future reality, you cast a clear vibrational message into that field—drawing opportunities, ideas, and synchronicities into alignment with your vision.

The Seeker's Awakening

The sage led the Seeker through their first authentic visualization.
"Close your eyes," he instructed, "and breathe deep. Now... envision the life you want. Not someday. Not tomorrow. But now."

And so the Seeker saw:

Their dream house, flooded with sunlight and peace.

Their body, strong, healthy, and full of vitality.

Their job, meaningful and fulfilling.

Their heart, filled with love and peace.

As the vision became sharper, feeling welled up—**not yearning, but thanksgiving.** They smiled, as though their dreams had already come.

In that instant, the Seeker knew:
What you see inside, you sow in the soil of the Universe. And with faith, it shall grow.

How to Visualize Effectively

The Seeker made visualization a daily practice. Here's what they discovered:

1. Create a Sacred Space:
Find a quiet spot where you won't be interrupted. Sit comfortably. Turn off the lights. Take deep breaths and let the present moment surround you.

2. Choose One Clear Desire:
Single-point your intention. Healing, abundance, relationship, clarity—clarity clarifies the signal.

3. Engage All Your Senses:
Visualize the colors. Listen to the sounds. Smell the scent. Feel the textures. The more tangible it feels, the more powerful the energetic imprint.

4. Engage Emotion:
Emotion is the pathway between thought and matter. Imagine as if your desire has already been met—joy, peace, pride, love.

5. Employ the Present Tense:
Imagine the vision as occurring right now. Not "I will be," but "I am."

6. Repetition Creates Momentum:
Consistency is the key. Imagine every day, particularly in the morning and at bedtime—when the mind is most receptive.

7. End with Gratitude:
Murmur "Thank you" as if already your reality is the vision. Gratitude completes the frequency of abundance.

The Mirror Effect

Before long, the Seeker started seeing signs.

A dialogue that reflected their vision.

A chance that harmonized with their dream.

A sudden inspiration to act on something they had visualized.

They weren't forcing their reality—they were becoming it.

Visualization didn't make the path easier; it made it visible. It gave the Seeker a map through the unseen terrain of their becoming.

Common Blocks to Visualization

The Seeker, like all of us, had to overcome a few challenges:

Doubt: "Is this just imagination?"
Answer: All creation begins in the imagination. Don't judge it. Trust the process.

Distractions: "My mind wanders."
Answer: It's okay. Gently bring your focus back. With
practice, the mind obeys.

Impatience: "Nothing is changing."
Answer: Seeds take time. Keep planting with faith. The
unseen is working.

Visualization Is Creation

The sage gave the Seeker one last truth:
"You are not just imagining a better life. You are teaching
the Universe to create it. The clearer you see it, the
quicker it comes."

And so, every day, the Seeker sat under the sky, eyes
closed but vision wide open.

They no longer dreamed of the life they desired.
They saw it. Believed it. Became it.
And the Universe did respond—not with miracles that
were beyond reach, but with dreams manifesting in their
hands.

See it. Feel it. Trust it.
Your inner world is the mold.
Your outer world is the reflection.

Gratitude

The Seeker once stood in the middle of a quiet forest, feeling lost. Though they had learned the laws of attraction, practiced visualization, and spoken affirmations, something still felt incomplete.

With a heavy heart, they sat beside a flowing stream and whispered to the sky,
"Why does it still feel like something is missing?"

Just then, the sound of the stream seemed to soften into a voice that spoke within:
"You ask, but do you thank? You wish, but do you see what's already here?"

And in that instant, the Seeker learned the secret bridge between wanting and getting—**Gratitude.**

Gratitude: The Most Magnetic Frequency

Gratitude is more than a feeling. It's a vibration.
It's the energetic signature of already having, already being, already becoming.

In the hidden language of the Universe, gratitude is the frequency that whispers:
"I already have enough. I already am enough. And I am open to more."

When you are thankful, you step out of lack and into abundance. You move from pursuing to receiving. You get in harmony with the very energy of the life you want.

The Seeker learned this principle:
Gratitude is not the effect of manifestation. It is the cause of it.

The Science Behind Gratitude

Gratitude rewires your brain. Neuroscience reveals that habitual gratitude:

Releases serotonin and dopamine, the happy chemicals.

Strengthens neural networks of positivity, optimism as a habit.

Reduces anxiety and stress, calming the nervous system and bringing clarity.

Activates the prefrontal cortex, planning, focus, and intention center.

Your mind changes, so does your reality.

The Spiritual Power of Thankfulness

From ancient writings to contemporary wisdom, all spiritual traditions acknowledge the power of thankfulness:

"Give thanks in all circumstances." —Bhagwat Gita

"Be grateful for whatever comes, because each has been sent as a guide." —Rumi

"Gratitude is the fairest blossom which springs from the soul." —Buddha

Gratitude is the language of the soul.
It blesses what is, with joyful anticipation of what's to be.

The Seeker's Daily Gratitude Ritual

Guided by the wise sage, the Seeker started each day with a humble but potent ritual:

Morning Gratitude Journal

Each morning upon waking, they wrote down:

1. Three things they were grateful for right now (family, breath, sunlight).

2. Two things they once desired that are now reality.

3. One thing not yet manifested—but written with gratitude as if it already was.

Example:

I'm so grateful for the peace in my heart.

I'm thankful for the opportunities that keep coming my way.

Thank you, Universe, for the financial abundance that flows to me easily.

This daily routine rewired the Seeker's mind from emptiness to abundance.
They ceased searching for reasons to be thankful—and began to create them.

The Shift Within

Days went by, and something shifted.

The Seeker no longer craved in desperation or frustration.
They smiled more, saw more, loved more.
Little things became holy—like the warmth of tea, the laugh of a stranger, the song of the wind.

And that inner delight... that deep satisfaction... became a magnet for more blessings.

Gratitude had opened the floodgates.

Gratitude for What's Yet to Come

The strongest expression of gratitude is this:
Thanking the Universe ahead of time.

When you're thankful before your dream has appeared,
you're giving a loud and clear message:
"I trust. I believe. I receive."

The Seeker wrote love letters to the future:

Thank you for the healing already taking place in my body.

Thank you for the soulmate who is making their way to me.

Thank you for the sacred timing of my dreams becoming a reality.

And slowly, those letters became actual chapters of their life.

When It's Hard to Feel Grateful

The Seeker experienced times of suffering too—loss, waiting, silence. But even during such dark times, the sage reminded:

"Gratitude is not about faking that everything is fine. It's about discovering light even in the shadow."

Even in struggle, the Seeker murmured:

I am thankful for the lesson in this suffering.

I am grateful for the strength of being born within me.

I am thankful that this too is part of my growth.

In doing so, even suffering became sacred.

Gratitude Changes Everything

The Seeker finally understood:
Gratitude doesn't just bring more to be thankful for—it changes you.

From fear to faith.
From resistance to flow.
From longing to peace.

You cease waiting for the miracle... and understand, you are already living within one.

End Practice: The Evening Gratitude Meditation

Every evening, the Seeker lay under the stars and whispered:

1. "Thank you for this breath."

2. "Thank you for the guidance I felt today."

3. "Thank you for what tomorrow is already preparing for me."

And as they slipped into slumber, they bore the vibration of abundance in their heart—seeding dreams in the Universe's soil.

Gratitude is not the end of your manifestation journey. It is the beginning, the middle, and the bridge to the end.
Be grateful—and watch the Universe pour more into your open hands.

"SURROUND YOURSELF WITH PEOPLE WHO BELIVE IN YOU MORE THAN YOU DO."

-NIHAL MUDGAL

Letting go

The Seeker had planted every seed.

They had dreamed with clarity, visualized with emotion, affirmed with conviction, and given thanks in advance. Yet as days turned into weeks, and weeks into months, doubt began to creep in.

One evening, under a moonlit sky, the Seeker returned to the old sage and asked:

"I've done everything. Why hasn't the Universe answered?"

The sage smiled gently and replied,
"Because your fists are still clenched. You're still trying to control what only surrender can unlock."

And so the Seeker learned the most holy and contradictory law of manifestation—**Letting Go**.

What Does It Mean to Let Go?

Letting go is not giving up.
It is not letting go of your desire or giving away your dreams.

It is releasing your attachment to how and when your desire will come into being.

**It is believing the process so much that you don't have
to understand, pursue, or plead anymore.**

Letting go is the ultimate act of faith.
It tells the Universe:
*"I trust you more than my timeline. I believe in your plan
more than my fears."*

The Illusion of Control

The Seeker came to an epiphany:
Their nervousness wasn't because the manifestation
wasn't occurring—
**It was because they were attempting to control the
result.**

And the harder they struggled to push it, the harder they
worked against themselves.

**In manifestation, control is resistance.
Letting go is flow.**

A river flows only when it does not have something
restricting it; otherwise, it pushes back, fighting its
confines.

Similarly, manifestation flows when we let go.

The Science of Letting Go

Psychology verifies what mystics thousands of years ago
already intuitively knew:
Letting go is a balanced mental and emotional state.

When you let go:

Cortisol levels fall, lowering stress levels.

**Your nervous system goes from survival to creation
mode** (parasympathetic activation).

The Reticular Activating System (RAS) in your brain
begins filtering in new possibilities without overanalysis.

You become receptive to serendipity, flow, and inspired
action.

Letting go aligns your inner world with ease. And the
Universe responds to that peace.

The Seeker's Shift

The sage gave the Seeker a feather and a stone.

"Carry both," he said.
"Hold the stone too tightly, and you'll feel its weight grow.
Hold the feather gently, and it will dance with the wind."

The Seeker smiled.

They understood:
Desires are like feathers—not meant to be clenched, but cradled in trust.

So they began to breathe deeper.
To smile more.
To act from inspiration, not desperation.
And most importantly—**to detach from the outcome.**

How to Practice Letting Go

Here's what the Seeker learned and practiced each day:

1. Recognize Your Attachments

Ask yourself:

Am I fixating on this want?

Am I fearing it won't come?

Do I feel less than if it doesn't come soon?

Awareness is the first freedom.

2. Transition from Need to Trust

Need is based on deficiency.
Trust is based on abundance.

Tell yourself:
"Even if it hasn't come yet, I'm already complete. I am safe. I trust divine timing."

3. Come back to the Now

Desperation exists in the future.
Peace exists in the now.

The Seeker discovered how to stay rooted in the here and now—through meditating, hiking, journaling, or merely observing clouds drifting by.

4. Inspired Action, Not Forced Action

Releasing does not equal inactivity.
It equals action that's guided by sense, ease, and joy—rather than driven by control or fear.

Pose, "What would my future self do today?"
And do that—with love, not compulsion.

5. Design a 'Let Go' Ritual

Every night, the Seeker penned their wishes on paper and softly said:

"I let go of this to the Universe. I know it's already mine."

And then they incinerated the paper or set it in the moonlight.
The practice was a reminder that letting go is holy.

When Letting Go Is Difficult

The Seeker encountered times of
uncertainty—questioning, waiting, wondering. But the
sage gently reminded: **"The tree doesn't tug on its fruit to
get it to ripen. It has faith in the sun, the earth, and the
seasons."** And so should we.

Letting go isn't a one-time thing. It's a daily decision—to
let go of worry and come back to faith.

The Paradox of Surrender

Shortly, something amazing occurred.

As the Seeker released...

Opportunities arose.

Answers showed up.

Paths unfolded.

Not when they forced it. But when they flowed.

That's the paradox:
The instant you let go, it begins to come.
The instant you are complete without it, it starts to arrive.
Because your vibration has become the match to your wish.

Surrender is not weakness.
It is power clothed in peace.
It is faith that the Universe knows the way— even when you can't see the map.

Final Wisdom

One evening, as the stars twinkled overhead, the Seeker whispered:
"I release. I receive. I trust."

And with that, they slept peacefully—not in worry, but harmony.

Not awaiting their dreams—
but evolving into the you that no longer has to wait.

Release.
Not because you don't care—
But because you care enough to trust the sacred timing of your life.

"I DIDN'T PUT THIS OBSTRACLE IN YOUR WAY TO STOP YOU. I PUT IT THERE TO REMIND YOU HOW POWERFUL YOU ARE." *-WHY UNIVERSE?*

CHAPTER THREE

INTERMEDIATE MANIFESTATION TECHNIQUES

The Seeker sat under the tree, heart peaceful, mind expanded. They knew the fundamentals of manifestation—the art of thought, intention, gratitude. Life was different now. Small desires started to show. But now something inside him tugged with an appetite new:

"I want to go deeper," the Seeker whispered to the wind.

"I want to control the unseen."

The Universe, ever listening, replied—not with a deafening voice, but subtle nudges of discernment.

And before long, three tools materialized on the Seeker's journey—**the Vision Board, Scripting, andManifestation Meditation.** These were not tricks of magic. **They were sacred tools—crossings from the inner realm to outer reality.**

Let us now venture into these tools that turn the whisper of the heart into the echo of the Universe.

1. Vision Board – Making the Invisible Visible

"What you can see every day, you begin to believe. And what you believe, you start to become."

The Seeker started with scissors, paper, and intention. They made a board—covered in pictures of dreams yet to be achieved: a lovely home, a joyful relationship, a thriving career, radiant health.

But this wasn't merely a collage.

It was a map of their future self.

A Vision Board is a physical or virtual assemblage of photos, words, and symbols for the reality that you are manifesting. It functions like a visual prayer, sending your needs to the subconscious mind and the field of endless possibilities.

How Vision Boards Work (The Science)

Activates the Reticular Activating System (RAS): assists the brain to filter in chances that align with your desires.

Neuroplasticity: The brain starts creating new paths based on repeated visualization.

Emotional Repetition: Repeated view generates emotional congruence, intensifying belief.

Steps to Create Your Vision Board

1. Clarify Your Desires: Be aware of what you desire in all realms—love, health, finances, expansion.

2. Gather Visuals: Utilize magazines, prints, or electronic boards such as Pinterest. Pick pictures that convey emotion.

3. Structure Creatively: Construct a design that feels motivational. Include affirmations or mantras.

4. Place with Purpose: Put your board in a place where you will see it every day—your desk, wall, or phone background.

5. Feel as You See: Not only look, but feel as if you are already living that life.

The Seeker's Realization

Days went by, and the Seeker no longer gazed at the vision board as a wish list, but as a confirmation.

"I am not hoping for this," they thought. "I am aligning with it."

2. Scripting – Writing Your Future into the Present

"The pen is a wand. Your journal is the altar. The words you write, if believed, will rise like smoke into the cosmos and return as form."

Scripting became the Seeker's nightly sacred ritual.

Every evening, they wrote in their journal and started with a potent statement:

"I am so happy and grateful now that..."

And then, they wrote. **They wrote of dreams as though they had occurred.**

With every page, the Seeker wasn't merely writing fantasy—they were rewiring their mind, changing identity, and establishing a vibrational alignment.

Why Scripting Works

Reprograms the Subconscious Mind: Informs the brain a new story, substitutes doubt with belief.

Triggers Emotion: Emotion strengthens manifestation. Writing in past/present tense brings real feelings.

Creates Identity Shift: You start behaving and believing as the version of yourself who already possesses it.

How to Script Effectively

1. Begin with Gratitude: It brings you into alignment with abundance.

"I'm so thankful that my business is booming and I feel successful."

2. Be Specific: Paint the picture, people, locations, feelings.

"This morning I woke up in my dream house, sunlight pouring in through huge windows. I feel peaceful and unencumbered."

3. Use Present/Past Tense: Write like it's already happening.

Avoid: "I want…"
Use: "I have…" or "I'm living…"

4. Revisit Often: Read your script aloud with feeling. Repetition builds belief.

The Seeker's Experience

After weeks of scripting, the Seeker noticed subtle changes.

They started walking taller. Speaking more confidently. Taking bolder steps.

The world hadn't changed yet.

But they had.

And because they changed, the world began to respond.

3. Meditation of Manifestation – Aligning Your Vibration

"When the mind is quiet, the soul communicates. And when the soul hums at the vibration of your wish, the world reorders itself to harmonize."

The last technique the Seeker was taught was the most internal—**Meditation for Manifestation.**

No longer simply sitting in quiet, now they went into meditation with intent:

To connect with their future now.

The Meditation Process

1. Sit in Stillness: Breathe deeply. Release the current moment's noise.

2. See Clearly: Picture your wish already granted. Be within the picture.

3. Use the Senses: What do you hear, see, smell, touch, taste?

4. Access the Emotion: Root in gratitude, peace, joy. Emotion is energy in motion.

5. Affirm Quietly: Whisper an inner affirmation such as "I am one with all I desire."

6. Release in Trust: Leave it in surrender. Let go of how and when.

Scientific Power of Meditation

-Changes Brain Waves: Transports you to alpha and theta levels—perfect for programming the subconscious.

-Strengthens Emotional Frequency: You become vibrational attunement to your goals.

-Reduces Resistance: Doubt and fear melt away in meditative calm.

The Seeker's Transformation

The Seeker felt lighter with every meditation. The hold of impatience relaxed.

They weren't waiting for manifestation.

They were becoming it.

In quiet, they heard a silent truth:

"The frequency you become is the life you attract."

Final Reflections: The Inner Alchemist

By practicing these intermediate techniques, the Seeker moved from wishing to embodying.
From thinking to believing.
From asking to receiving.

These tools are not to be rushed or mechanically repeated.
They are invitations—to become the version of yourself who is ready to receive.

Vision Boards make your dreams visible.
Scripting makes your dreams believable.
Meditation makes your dreams vibrational.

When all three are accomplished in faith, with happiness, and without hopelessness—**the Universe always gives back.**

SOMETIMES THE THINGS YOU'RE AFRAID OF DOING ARE THE VERY IMPORTANT THINGS THAT WILL SET YOU FREE." -NIHAL MUDGAL

Vision Board

The Seeker walked along a silent forest at dawn. Yellow light poured between the trees, and the air vibrated with quiet. The path of inner change had shown them much truth, but this morning, the Universe whispered a new truth:

"You must now see what you wish to become."

The Seeker hesitated. "I see it in my head," they said.

The leaves whispered among themselves like laughter. **"See it in your world."**

And so, the next tool on the Seeker's path revealed itself—**a Vision Board**. A sacred space to bring dreams out of the mind and into the material.

What Is a Vision Board?

A Vision Board is a physical or digital collection of images, affirmations, words, and symbols that represent your desires. But more than that—it is a mirror of your future, a creative altar that reflects your highest intentions.

It's not all about cutting out images and sticking them up. It's about deliberately creating the energy of your desired reality so that your subconscious mind starts believing, and your life starts to change.

The Science of Vision Boards

The Seeker sat next to the sage, who now answered not in mysticism, but in science.

"What you see on a daily basis, your brain starts to perceive as familiar. And what becomes familiar becomes possible."

Here's how:

-Reticular Activating System (RAS): This component of your brain screens information and pays attention to what you care about. When your wishes are visually before you each day, your RAS starts scanning the world for similar opportunities.

-Neuroplasticity: Consistent visualization reprograms the brain. Your neurons start firing in sync with the vision, strengthening new behaviors and beliefs.

-Emotional Encoding: Pictures stir emotion, and emotion is energy. This emotional vibration is what the Universe answers. The more you feel connected to your vision, the quicker it materializes.

Creating Your Vision Board: A Sacred Ritual

When the Seeker began creating their vision board, it wasn't simply a creative endeavor—it became a ritual. A meditative instant of alignment. A ritual of embodiment.

Here's how you can make your own:

Step 1: Clarify Your Desires

Grab a journal and think deeply.
What do you really want in these areas?

-**Health:** How do you want to feel in your body?

-**Relationships:** What type of love is around you?

-**Career/Wealth:** What does success and abundance look like?

-**Spirituality:** What type of peace or connection are you looking for?

-**Lifestyle:** Where do you reside? How do you get around? What makes you happy?

Let your heart respond—not your fears or conditioning.

Step 2: Collect Visuals and Words

Look at pictures online, in magazines, or even create your own. Select images that speak to emotion, not reason. If a picture **evokes happiness or desire**—that's your cue.

Include as well:

-Affirmations

-Words of encouragement that motivate you

-Symbols or sacred geometry

-Pictures of your desired future self

Step 3: Create with Purpose

As you set each image, sense the feeling of already possessing it. Your energy in creating the board is more important than its aesthetic quality.

Set love quotes beneath pictures of couples. Set affirmations beside a dream house. Stack pictures that resonate with your soul.

This is your manifestation altar. Treat it with respect.

Step 4: Set It Where You'll See It Often

The Seeker put their board next to their bed. Every morning and evening, they looked at it—not as a wish list, but as **a reminder of what was already theirs vibrationally.**

You can put your vision board:

-On a wall you see every day

-In your office

-As your phone or desktop wallpaper

-Inside a journal (for a portable one)

Activating the Board with Energy

After your board is made, bring it to life.

Visualize Daily: Take a few minutes each day to imagine yourself within the board.

Feel the Emotions: Happiness, thankfulness, self-assurance, and calmness.

Speak Affirmations Out Loud: "This is my life. I am experiencing this now."

Express Gratitude: As though you've already received it.

Your vision board is not a fixed collage—**it's a living energy field. It changes with you.**

The Seeker's Experience

Weeks went by. The Seeker didn't merely glance at the board—they became it.

When they saw an image of a best-seller, they started writing with affection. When they saw a vision of radiant health, they started taking care of their body.

Then the miracles happened.

-An offer to publish came out of the blue.

-A soulmate walked into their life.

-Their energy started to radiate like the picture they had pinned up.

The Seeker smiled.
"I didn't pursue my vision. I embodied it. And it came."

"The power of a vision board is not in the pictures. It's in the frequency you emit when you look at them."

"It is a doorway—not to the future, but to the version of you who already lives that future."

Final Reflections

A vision board is a reminder to live in alignment—not in anxiety. To act with faith, not fear. To become magnetic rather than desperate.

It is a call each day to recall:

-*Who you are becoming*

-*What you really want*

-*And how strong your inner world actually is*

**The Seeker's board now radiates more than pictures.
It radiates faith.**

And so can yours.

"EVEN DELAYS ARE BLESSINGS TRUST ME."

-WHY UNIVERSE?

Scripting

The night was still. There was a flicker of a candle burning. The Seeker sat with a journal, hand on page, heart open and mind searching. They were familiar with manifestation, they had practiced with gratitude, and they had envisioned their desires. But the Universe now breathed to them:

"Your words are wands. Write with faith. Write as if it already is."

And so they began to write.

Not out of desperation. Not out of hope. But because they knew.

Know that the process of writing was not merely ink on paper. It was the process of taking energy form.

What Is Scripting?

Scripting is putting your desires into written form as if they've already happened. It's manifestation in the form of a story—your story, written beforehand.

You are the author of your destiny. Your journal is the canvas upon which your destiny is written.
Scripting is different from journaling. It is intentional, sensory, present tense storytelling that prepares your

subconscious mind for a new reality.

The Seeker's First Script

The Seeker opened up their journal and wrote: *"I'm so thankful and happy now that I wake up every morning feeling rich and whole. My book is a global bestseller. People send me messages every day telling me how their lives have transformed. I feel whole, strong, and profoundly at peace."*

They didn't just write it.

They **felt** it.
They **saw** it.
They **believed** it.

Why Scripting Works (The Science and Psychology)

-**Subconscious Programming:** The brain is unable to distinguish between what is and consciously imagined events. As you write, you're seeding new patterns of belief into the subconscious, which controls over 90% of everything you do.

-**Law of Attraction Activation:** Writing in present tense guarantees that you align your energy with what you want. The Universe responds to the frequency.

-**Neuroplasticity:** Ongoing positive scripting creates new neural pathways, replacing power-depleting negative thinking with empowering attitudes.

-**Emotion + Imagination** = Manifestation: The written word activates imagination, and put together with emotion, it's a creation magnet.

How to Script Effectively

Let this not be a dry exercise. Create ritual.

1. Set the Scene

Choose a peaceful moment. Light a candle. Put on soothing music. Make scripting a moment of communion with the future you.

2. Start with Gratitude

Begin every script with appreciation—it opens the heart and raises your frequency.

"I'm so thankful for the peace and love I have in my life every day."

3. Use Present or Past Tense

Script as though your desire has already happened.

Don't script: "I hope I get a job."
I'm so thankful for my amazing job that inspires and fulfills
me."

4. Be Descriptive and Emotional

Use sensory language. Make the reader (you) touch and
feel each word.

"I went into my new house today. The smell of lavender
welcomed me. The sun kissed every corner. I felt. home."

5. Emphasize the Feeling

What would your future self be feeling? Joy? Confidence?
Freedom? Write that into your script.

"As I stood on stage, speaking to thousands, my heart was
full of purpose."

6. Repetition is Power

Write every day or a week. Read old scripts. Rewrite
them with new clarity. Let your reality shift on the
page.

Pitfalls to Avoid

-Writing from Lack:*Avoid writing from what you don't*
want, or what you lack.
Instead of: "I'm no longer broke," say: "I love the financial

-Overthinking the 'How': Your job is the what and why. Leave the how to the Universe.

-Doubt and Hesitation: Scripting works only if you believe. Even when you don't, just write anyway. Let faith build up through repetition.

The Seeker's Shift

Where weeks turned into days, scripting became the Seeker's closest practice.
Not just for making their desires manifest,
But for becoming their future self.

They did not just want change.
They scripted themselves into change.

One evening, as they read over an old script, they gasped—it had all materialized. Word for word. Feeling for feeling. Reality had reordered itself.

The tale they once conjured, they were now living.

Advanced Scripting Tips

-Write a Letter to Yourself: From your future self, reflecting on all that you have brought into being.

-**Script a Perfect Day:** Morning to evening, write about how your ideal life feels.

-**Use "I Am" Statements:** Powerful builders of identity.

"I am worthy. I am aligned. I am receiving."

-**Burn or Release Old Scripts:** Let go of old ways of being that no longer serve your highest vision.

The Sacred Power of Words

Words are energy. And energy is creation.
The Seeker then understood that the Universe not only hears what you say—but what you intentionally write.
Every word a strand in the fabric of their destiny.

If you wish to alter your life," the sage had instructed them, "alter your story first."

They wrote.
And their story was set free.

Meditation For Manifestation

"When Stillness Speaks, The Universe Listens"

The world outside was loud. Thoughts ran, doubts whispered, and desires screamed for attention. The Seeker sat quietly, eyes closed, breath calm. Not to escape—but to **align.**

For it was in quiet, the Universe spoke the loudest. And it was in that quiet, manifestation accelerated.

"Be still," the sage had said,
"for the frequency of all creation is born from inner peace."

And so, the Seeker moved inward—to create not through force, but through resonance.

Why Meditation Matters in Manifestation

Manifestation isn't about thinking happy thoughts or visualizing what you want—it's about becoming the energetic match to what you're looking to create.

But how do you match up with abundance when your mind is noisy?

Meditation clears the static.
It breaks down resistance.
It returns you to your natural, receptive state—the place where the Universe moves through you.

The Science of Manifestation Meditation

1. Brainwave Shift

Your brain during meditation switches **from beta (stress) to alpha and theta (relaxed, creative) frequencies.**
These brainwaves are best suited for:

Reprogramming the subconscious

Tapping into imagination

Emotional depth visualizing

2. Heart-Brain Coherence

Meditation aligns your heart rhythm with your brain, generating **coherence**—a highly potent state in which intention and emotion unite, and your body is made a magnet for manifestation.

3. Cortisol Reduction = Higher Vibration

When you meditate, cortisol (stress hormone) falls. Your vibration increases. You radiate frequencies of love, peace, gratitude—the same vibrations your desires reside on.

"You don't attract what you want. You attract what you are."
Meditation allows you to become what you want.

The Seeker's First Meditation

The Seeker sat under a tree, barefoot and indecisive.
Could stillness truly bring change?

They breathed.
And again.
And gradually, the chatter subsided.
Their mind became a mirror.
And in that mirror, they saw it all:

-The home they envisioned

-The laughter of their beloved

-The purpose burning in their chest

-The abundance already present

They didn't ask.
They didn't beg.
They just became.

And that was enough.

Various Forms of Manifestation Meditation

There is no single way. The Seeker found many.

1. Visualization Meditation

-Close your eyes.

-Imagine your desire already manifest.

-See, hear, feel every detail.

-Let emotion flood your body.

Pro Tip: *Do this when just waking or going to sleep—when your subconscious is most receptive.*

2. Affirmation Meditation

-Sit quietly.

-Silently or out loud, repeat such affirmations as:

I am worthy.

I am already living my dream.

Everything I desire flows to me effortlessly.

-Feel each word's truth in your body.

3. Breath-Focused Meditation (To Release Resistance)

-Breathe in for 4 counts, hold for 4, exhale for 4.

-As you breathe, silently repeat:

-With each breath, I align.

-With every exhale, I let go of doubt.

This soothes the nervous system and creates room for receiving.

4. Guided Manifestation Meditations

Employ recorded meditations on abundance, success, love, or healing. The Seeker would often listen to one before bed—nourishing their subconscious with new truths while they slept.

How Long and How Often?

There are no hard and fast rules—but consistency is crucial.

-10–15 minutes a day can change your frequency.

-Mornings are most powerful—set your vibration before the day starts.

-Even one deep breath with intention is powerful.

The Seeker's Awakening

Months into the practice, something changed.

Not outside—yet.
But inside.

They no longer needed to manifest to prove their worth.
They meditated because they remembered they were
already whole.

And that wholeness?
It manifested love, opportunities, money,
healing—without chase.

**"Stillness," the sage said, "is the shortcut you've been
searching for."**

Your Manifestation Meditation Ritual

1. Create Sacred Space:
Light a candle. Play soft frequencies. Make the energy feel
pure.

2. Set an Intention:
What are you aligning to today? Peace? Wealth? Love?

3. Enter the Silence:
Work with breath, visualization, or affirmation.

4. Feel It in Your Cells:
Don't just look at your desire—be it.

5. Close with Gratitude:
Say thank you. Not as ritual—but as truth.

Final Reflection

Manifestation meditation is not about getting—it's about
aligning.
It is the door to your higher self.
It is the place where desires are no longer desired—but
received.

The Seeker now sits in meditation not to draw in more,
but to recall more of who they are:
A soul of boundless potential.
A magnet of creation.
A being in complete harmony with the Universe.

And so are you.

CHAPTER FOUR

RISING ABOVE CHALLENGES IN MANIFESTATION

"The Storm Before the Shift – When the Universe Tests the One It Trusts Most"

The Seeker had walked a long path—through intentions, visualizations, scripting, meditation, and surrender. They had planted seeds of faith in the soil of their soul.

But then came the drought.

Suddenly, the affirmations felt empty.

The visualizations blurred.

Doubt returned like an old, uninvited guest.

"Why is nothing happening?" the Seeker cried to the stars.

"I've done everything."

And then, in the stillness that lingered, a voice whispered from the Universe:

"This is not punishment. This is purification."

The Nature of Challenges During Manifestation

As you set an intention to manifest something incredible, you're not just creating a outcome—**you're summoning change.**

And change requires one thing more than anything else: **A change in identity.**

Your present self must dissolve so that the creation you've wanted can be contained by the new you.

That dissolution always appears as chaos.

-Things fall apart.

-People leave.

-Money depletes.

-Feelings swell like wild waves.

But this is not devastation. It is rebuilding.

Why the Universe Tests You

You're not being tested to decide whether or not you're worthy.

You're being refined **to realize that you already are.**

Challenges arise to:

-Strengthen your vibration

-Clear limiting beliefs

-Shatter attachment to control

-Teach surrender

-Develop emotional resilience

It's resistance training for the soul.

The Universe never presents you with difficulty to hold you back. It presents you with friction to help you **forge alignment.**

The Seeker's Dark Night

There was a moment when nothing was right for the Seeker.

They had written from love, prayed in faith, beheld their dreams every day.

But instead of forward motion, there was stop. Silence. Even suffering.

First, they tried to get the Universe to respond.

But manifestation is not forced. It is allowed.

So, in desperation, they finally did what they dreaded most to do:

They released.

Not the dream. But the desperation.

And in that letting go, the Universe shifted.

Because sometimes, your greatest strength is not in effort—but in trust.

Common Obstacles along the Path of Manifestation

Let's find out what tends to come up—and how to rise above each.

1. Doubt and Fear

When results take their time to show, the mind panics: "Maybe this doesn't work."

How to lift:

Back to silence and meditation.

Read your journals and past scripts again.

Affirm: "What I want is coming, even when I can't yet see it."

2. Negative Outside Situations

You might lose a job first before you achieve your dream one.

A love relationship might end before your soulmate arrives.

Why?

Because the Universe gets rid of the wreckage before the miracle.

How to transcend:

Have faith in the detour. All loss is hidden harmonization.

Look at what's being made, not what's lost.

3. Impatience

Time lag generates discouragement. But remember: The bamboo tree takes years to grow underground before growing 90 feet in weeks.

How to move above:

Release deadlines.

Say again: "Divine timing is always perfect."

Use delays as time to get ready for your new life.

4. Emotional Setbacks

Past traumas, insecurities, and wounds may surface.

This isn't regression. It's release.

You're being asked to let go of emotional weight that cannot travel to your next level.

How to rise above:

Allow emotions to flow without judgment.

Journal. Seek healing. Cry. Breathe. Trust.

The Power of Inner Resilience

Manifestation is not about pretending to be perfect. It's about being real, staying aligned, and showing up even when it's hard.

Resilience is the connection between intention and outcome.

The Seeker found that the greatest shifts always came after their most full-scale breakdowns.

Since manifestation isn't actually about requesting from the Universe to have more—it's about embodying more of you.

Practical Steps When in Crisis

1. Ground Yourself in the Now:
Breathe deeply. Plant roots in now.
Now is always secure.

2. Re-COMMIT to Your Practice:
Go back to your practices—meditation, gratitude, scripting. Don't leave the tools that increased your vibration to begin with behind.

3. Find Community and Support:
Talk to trusted hearts who understand. Healing compounds in collective energy.

4. Learn from Your Triggers:
What's bubbling up in your inner landscape? These are clues to where alignment still needs nurturing.

5. Ask Better Questions:
Instead of "Why is this happening to me?" ask:
"What is this here to teach me?"

The Seeker's Breakthrough

One evening, after a day that had pierced so deeply, the Seeker sat beside a river. Tears in their eyes, but faith in their heart.

They didn't plead for answers.
They didn't seek signs.

They merely whispered:
"I trust. Even now."

And in that stillness, something shifted. Not out there, but in here.

A sense of peace.
Of power.
Of knowing.

And then the expressions began showing up—not because they were spotless, but because they had coordinated finally with trust.

Your Challenge is Sacred

You are not lost.
You are not forsaken.
You are not faltering.
You are rising.
All challenges are gateways.
All detours are guides.
All breakdowns are initiations.

The Seeker was created because they made a choice between trust and fear.

And now so will you.

"The Universe doesn't test you to see if you can survive."

It tests you so you remember you are invincible.

You are not just manifesting things.

You are manifesting yourself—the best version.

The real you.

"IF YOU COULD SEE WHAT I SEE. YOU'D STOP WORRING AND START CELEBRATING."

-WHY UNIVERSE?

Dealing with Doubt and Fear

The Seeker had come a long way. From intending to meditating for clearness, from writing out desires to letting go of outcomes—they had traveled far. But with all their discipline and belief, an inner turmoil started to brew. Doubt crept in like a cold, slow fog. It wasn't loud or showy. It whispered softly in the silences, "What if this does not work? " And once that whisper echoed, fear found its way in too.

"What if I'm not worthy?

" "What if I'm simply not enough? " This is where most give up. When the very act that was once full of promise starts to seem like a question mark. The Seeker also stood at this edge, wondering whether to hold on or release. But something within them—a deeper knowing than thought—pushed them to continue walking. Doubt and fear were not indicators of failure. They were indicators that something was being awakened, unearthed, and exposed. In reality, doubt is the mind's old protector. It emerges from ancient memories, from previous disappointments and inherited assumptions, to inquire, "Are we safe?

" It is the whisper of times you attempted and came up short, or were made to feel insignificant for desiring too much.

Fear, however, is not always boisterous or overt. It usually disguises itself in fear, in delay, in the insidious self-destruction that comes after an act of courage. It is the nervous system recalling every hurtful moment, and cautioning you against returning to it. But manifestation isn't something that occurs on the surface. It isn't merely a matter of being positive and using the right words. It is a deep reformation of who you are, and the old you will fight that. Fear and doubt bubble up because part of you still holds on to the known—even if that known is limitation. The Seeker didn't flee from their fear. They sat with it.

One night, under a dark sky crowded with far-off stars, they shut their eyes and asked themselves: "What am I truly afraid of?

" And the responses emerged slowly, not as rational conclusions, but as profound emotional truths.

They were afraid of being seen.

They were afraid of being disappointed.

They were afraid that, if it didn't happen, it would validate the soft voice inside that had always said, "You don't deserve it."

But the Seeker also came to understand something powerful—fear and doubt weren't enemies. They were messages. They were teachers. Their presence didn't indicate the path was incorrect; it indicated something within was being called into healing. They were echoes of the past, requesting love, understanding, and freedom.

With every breath, the Seeker started talking to those aspects of themselves. Not to shut them up, but to calm them down. "I see you," they said to the fear. "But you no longer own me." And bit by bit, that fear relaxed. It didn't disappear altogether—it changed. It evolved into courage in disguise. Courage, after all, is not the absence of fear, but the willingness to act despite it. Through this internal work, the Seeker came to understand a deeper truth: the manifestation process isn't a straight line. It's a cycle. It includes light and dark, clarity and confusion, faith and doubt. All big dreams necessitate the dreamer letting go of old skin. And those old skins don't leave quietly—they fight. That fight is not a blockage, it's a passage. They also discovered that fear is stored in the body as tension, unease, and emotional triggers. When they breathed deep and were present, they could sense the hold of fear relaxing. When they wrote down their thoughts, the turmoil of their inner universe started to get sorted. When they refocused on their vision—what they really wanted and why it was important to them—they recalled their purpose, and purpose left fear with less space to occupy. As time went on, fear would still come around, but its voice became softer. Doubt would still ring out, but it could no longer dictate truth. What got louder was the soul's clarity, the heart's knowing, the whisper of intuition that said, "You're exactly where you need to be. The Seeker came out of this inner conflict not as one who had overcome fear, but as one who had learned to walk alongside it, unshaken. They had turned doubt into determination, fear into faith, and resistance into resilience. And with that, the way ahead opened once more—not because all uncertainty disappeared, but because they had become strong enough to walk through it. The Universe doesn't demand perfection. It doesn't hold you until you are fearless. It just invites you to be present—where you are—and to keep making choices for faith, over and over. Fear and doubt may visit, but they don't get to stay. And as the Seeker now knew, when you no longer fear the darkness inside you, your light burns all the brighter.

YOUR PATH MAY TWIST,

BUT IT'S NEVER WRONG. -*WHY UNIVERSE?*

Breaking Limiting Beliefs

"The Quiet Walls Inside – And the Force to Break Through Them"

Far had the Seeker gone, traveling down the path of intent and precision. They had conquered fear, embodied stillness, and become intimate with the vibrations of their deepest desires. Yet, with everything they had achieved, a muted frustration persisted—a quiet thing stopped them from continuing. No matter how strongly they could picture their visions, how loudly they proclaimed them, or how profoundly they immersed, the outcome appeared tardy or diluted. There seemed an impenetrable barrier in front of them between where they stood and where they wanted to bring things to life.

During a certain night, amidst calmness under an unperturbed sky, there emerged from inside them a gentle whisper: **"You don't deserve it."**
They stung like a flash. Basic. Gentle. Yet shattering.

In that moment, the Seeker realized the truth. The barrier wasn't outside. It wasn't time or fate or failure. It was belief.

Limiting beliefs are quiet designers of reality. They don't yell. They don't bicker. They just exist behind the scenes, molding the frame in which we view the world. They mutter from the shadows, "This is simply the way it is," or

"People like you don't get to do that." And the horror is, we think they're true—not because they are, but because they sound like something we've heard before.

These are the beliefs that we tend to inherit before we even realize we've adopted them. Passed down from family, culture, early life, and even from past traumas. The child who hears, "Money doesn't grow on trees," grows up to feel guilty about wealth. The one who heard, "Love always ends in pain," automatically repels connection. The one who was told, "You're not smart enough," later hesitates to pursue their dreams.

Inner glass ceilings are the result of limiting beliefs. You can look over them and observe others succeeding, flourishing, living without constraints—but whatever you do, something prevents you from joining them. Not that you're not capable, but because your subconscious thinks that safety lies only below that ceiling.

For the Seeker, this was both a painful and a freeing moment. Painful, in that it showed just how much of their pain had originated from within. Liberating, in that it meant that the ability to change was within as well.

They started the deep work—not of manifesting more, but of unlearning the invisible rules that had ruled their life. They went back to their journal and inquired mighty questions: What do I really think about myself? About love? About success? About worthiness? The responses trickled in at first, hidden under layers of spiritual bypassing and positive thinking. But with time, the truth revealed itself.

They understood that they believed it was selfish to ask for more. That happiness had to be earned by suffering. That their value was based on productivity. These were not facts—these were old stories. But until those stories were active, everything was shaped by them.

To move them, the Seeker needed to do more than merely repeat affirmations. They needed to embody them. To confront them. To create evidence against them. With every action against an old thought—spoke their truth, received without shame, rested without guilt—they shattered the illusion further. Neuroplasticity, the brain's capacity to rewire itself, was no longer theory—it was their lived experience.

The Seeker also started paying attention to how their body reacted to these beliefs. When they dwelled on abundance, their chest would constrict. When they dwelled on success, worry would swell up. So they went to breath, to stillness, to body awareness. They breathed safety into the pockets where fear once resided. They imagined new iterations of themselves—confident, loved, boundless—and allowed their nervous system to become comfortable with those futures.

Slowly, the inner walls began to crumble. The beliefs that once felt so absolute lost their grip. A deeper voice emerged, one not forged in fear but born from truth. It whispered, "You are worthy just by being." "Joy is your birthright." "There is no virtue in suffering."

And in this new light, manifestation transformed. It was no longer about struggling or repairing—it was about revealing what was always present when the self is in harmony with truth. The external world began to mirror this transformation. Opportunities abounded. Relationships became more profound. Peace filled the old gap of lack.

The Seeker discovered that shattering limiting beliefs is not a single action—it is a process of rebirth. Each time we encounter a new edge, a new dream, a new level of expansion, the old beliefs come back to be tested. But now, they possessed the tools. The awareness. The courage. They had become their own liberator.

So if you, as the Seeker, feel stuck in spite of your best efforts—stop. Don't press harder. Turn inward instead. What do you really think you can do? What are you still afraid to own? What story have you believed as true?

Because the truth is, you were never confined—just your belief was. And when you start to notice that, to question that, to redraft that... the walls come tumbling down. And your universe gets bigger with them.

"EMBRACE THE CHAOS.

IT'S BIRTHPLACE OF TRANSFORMATION."

-WHY UNIVERSE?

Persistence and Patience

"The Enduring Dance of Will and Surrender"

There was a point in the Seeker's path when it seemed that time itself had come to a stop. The affirmations were steady, the visualizations bright, the meditations profound, and the heart expansive—but yet, the manifestation they had so clearly envisioned in their mind's eye hadn't materialized. Weeks became months, and months became weeks. That initial excitement began to dwindle like mist in the sunlight. Doubt crept in once more, and silence rang out louder than ever.

It was in that quiet, this uneasy and unfamiliar place, that the Seeker came to comprehend two of the most misconceived yet divine energies of manifestation: persistence and patience. Not the kind that derives from sheer force of will or coerced positive thinking, but the kind born of soul understanding and divine faith. Persistence is the commitment to remain the path even when evidence is not. Patience is the elegance to wait without breaking, understanding that time does not postpone what is destined—it readies you for it.

The Illusion of Instant Gratification

In an instant-gratification world conditioned by overnight success, instant results, and speedy validation, waiting has been confused with stagnation. But real creation—spiritual, transformative creation—does not have a clock. It progresses in harmony with energy, emotion, alignment, and divine timing. As seeds under the ground, your wishes are establishing roots long before they flower on top. And if you uncover them too early to see how they're getting along, you break the very magic that was working behind the scenes on your behalf.

The Seeker must learn that delay was not denial—it was refinement. The Universe never responds with "no" to your wantings when they're in alignment with your soul. But instead, it usually says, "Not yet. Become the version of yourself who can contain this without fear. Grow first, receive second."

The Spiritual Nature of Persistence

Persistence is not resistance. It isn't pushing or striving or forcing life to your desire. It is presence. It is the choice to continue aligning, even when there isn't physical evidence. It is getting up each morning and behaving as though your manifestation is a done deal, because in the energy world—it already is.

Each time the Seeker came back to their vision board, not with desperation but devotion, they were declaring their faith in the process. Each script they wrote, each meditation they did, each time they opted for faith over fear—they were grounding into the frequency of their desired reality. They knew manifestation wasn't a one-time ask and wait. It was about becoming a living embodiment of the result, repeatedly, until the outside world had no other option but to reflect it back.

Persistence is also maintaining course when you're tested. And you'll be tested. Not by the Universe to penalize you, but by your own subconscious mind to demonstrate that you're serious. Every setback is not failure—it's a checkpoint. A time that inquires: Will you take the old self or the new? Will you fall or grow? Will you act or respond wisely?

And in those moments, persistence is holy. Because it no longer stems from fear or desperation—it stems from belief.

The Gentle Power of Patience

If persistence is fire, patience is water. It is the calm lake that mirrors the sky. It is the breathing after the storm. Patience is not passive—it is strong. It is, "I trust that what is meant for me will never miss me." It doesn't struggle against the current, it rides with it.

The Seeker came to know that lack of patience was an act of not believing. Such a little indication to the Universe: I do not think that it works. But patience countered, I have it in mind already; the physical merely catches up on a while after.

They started living their days, not as one who was in need, but as one who was preparing. They tidied up their house as if guests were already coming. They cared for their body as if already successful. They spoke as if having already arrived. This wasn't delusion—it was alignment.

The irony is that when you're no longer desperate for it to come in, it does come in. Why? Because you are no longer pushing against it. You've become a vibrational match through letting go, not insisting.

When Nothing is Happening, Everything is Happening

There were days when the Seeker felt they were spinning around in circles. When meditation seemed empty, when writing was unnatural, when signs failed to appear. But they realized that spiritual work isn't always spectacular. Sometimes it is quiet, monotonous, and repetitive. It is these times when your roots develop deeply.

Imagine the bamboo plant that grows years and years underground before it ever so much as rips through. But when it does, within weeks it stands several feet high.

This is manifestation energy. What is hidden is most powerful. Development done in the non-seein' is where miracles in the seein' are built upon.

The Seeker started to celebrate this secret work. They celebrated the quiet days, the slow days, the days that seemed like nothing. Because they finally knew: if you are steady in your energy, the Universe is steady in its orchestration.

Inner Transformation Before Outer Manifestation

One night, writing by candlelight, the Seeker penned something deep: "What if I'm not here to get something, but to become someone?"

That one changed everything.

They had always thought manifestation was about stuff—it was about change. The house, the relationship, the wealth—they're indicators of your growth. The real miracle is who you're becoming in the process. Who you're becoming when you endure through darkness. Who you're becoming when you decide on faith amidst chaos. Who you're becoming when you wait in grace.

Every moment of patience is a lesson in mastering emotions. Every persistent action is a message to your soul that you're prepared. And gradually, day by day, you cease chasing and begin attracting. Because your energy no longer whispers "I need," it whispers "I am."

The Universe Listens to Energy, Not Time

This became a fundamental truth to the Seeker: the Universe is not paying attention to the clock—it's tuning into your frequency.

When your internal world is rich with trust, gratitude, joy, and peace, it doesn't matter how long something takes—you feel the reality within you. And this internal embodiment shortens the external timeline. Not because you forced it, but because you no longer need it to complete you.

The Seeker released deadlines. They relinquished expectations. They existed in a sense of divine timing, knowing that everything either shows up at the right time or arrives as a lesson getting you ready for something bigger.

And in that letting go, life started surprising them. Random calls, synchronicities, spontaneous insights. It wasn't magic—it was momentum finally manifest.

Embracing the Journey

Patience and persistence are not enemies—they're allies. One has the vision, the other has the space. Together, they make manifestation a transformation, not a transaction.

The Seeker, previously restless, now had peace with progress even when unseen. They believed that every step counted, even when the road curved. They no longer dreaded time—they embraced it. For they understood time wasn't set against them—it was set alongside them.

This new beat brought peace. The necessity to control dissipated. The sense of urgency softened. In its stead emerged a still confidence—an unshakeable understanding that what was intended would arrive, and that they were becoming more than prepared to receive it.

Because ultimately, the true question was never "How quickly will it arrive?" The true question was, "Who am I becoming while I wait?"

And the Seeker had become lovely: a person who no longer pursued miracles—because they had become one.

Handling Setbacks

"The Holy Alchemy of Disappointment and Redirect"

The Seeker sat beside the window, eyes staring out to the horizon as storm clouds built up over the far-off hills. The air outside was heavy, not only with the impending rain but with an unspoken sorrow that was reflected in the quiet in here. This wasn't the first time the Seeker felt this burden—this pain of a dream that failed to materialize, of plans that went awry, of efforts that met little or nothing in return.

There had been setbacks before, and each time, they came like uninvited guests. They knocked not only on the doors of destiny but on the doors of the heart. And every time, they carried with them questions the mind was not always prepared to confront: Why did this occur? What am I doing wrong? Is the Universe ignoring me?

But during this chapter of their adventure, the Seeker started to discover something more: that failure was not the end. That it was pauses. Redirects. Wake-up calls. And occasionally—sometimes"—sometimes"—they were sacred detours crafted by the Universe to bring the soul back into balance.

The Illusion of Failure

In the beginning of their manifestation process, the Seeker thought that each failure was a misstep, a defect in their process. A lost opportunity was punishment, a missed chance personal defeat. But with time—and suffering—they came to understand that what seems like failure from the ego's narrow perspective is often divine design from the higher self.

The Universe does not operate according to human logic. Its intelligence is a far cry from what the mind can process. What looks like a wait could be protection. What looks like rejection could be redirection. What looks like a closed door could be the wrong house entirely.

The Seeker needed to release the requirement that they could only call each experience "good" or "bad." They started asking improved questions—not "Why me?" but "What is this trying to teach me?" Not "What did I lose?" but "What am I being prepared for?"

Emotional Alchemy: From Breakdown to Breakthrough

Setbacks are raw. They hurt. They are perplexing. They can create a loop of fear, self-doubt, and desperation. But these feelings are not the enemy—they are energy. And when energy is recognized, respected, and worked through with love, it is changed. This is emotional alchemy.

The Seeker learned to accommodate the pain, but not stifle it. They cried when they had to. They screamed at the night sky when silence felt too cacophonous. They wrote their outrage, their grief, their bewilderment. They voiced their feelings, and in that process, gave them an exit.

Healing starts not with denial, but with honesty. And the honesty was—sometimes things hurt. Sometimes life isn't fair. Sometimes the inner work still doesn't bring instant fruit. But the grace of emotional alchemy is this: what begins as heartbreak can become wisdom. What starts as grief can become grace.

In the stillness after the storm, the Seeker would always hear a whisper from the Universe: You are not broken. You are being rebuilt.

Lessons Hidden in the Rubble

Each setback contains a secret. A coded message. A lesson shrouded in disappointment. The Seeker started to ask themselves in each moment of adversity: What is the Universe revealing to me now?

Oftentimes the reply was clarity—an understanding that what they were after wasn't ultimately in line with their soul's intention.

Sometimes it was humility—an opportunity to let go of the ego timeline and become further entrenched in faith. Sometimes it was strength—for only in pushing through can we awaken the latent abilities within.

The way of manifestation is not about being pain-free. It's about employing pain as a gateway to change.

The Seeker realized that setbacks weren't detours along the path—they were the path. The ground of disappointment became the soil where their resilience took root.

The Role of the Subconscious and Setbacks

Most setbacks occur not because of external circumstances but because of internal resistance. The subconscious mind, conditioned with limiting beliefs during childhood, tends to sabotage progress not out of evil intent but out of fear.

The Seeker started to reveal hidden patterns:

-A fear of success disguised as procrastination.

-An unworthiness wound that shut down receiving.

-A conviction that struggle was more spiritual than ease.

Not every setback became a chance to look at the shadows within. Not to shame themselves, but to reclaim power. They learned to reprogram their subconscious by using daily affirmations, visualization, inner child work, and forgiveness.

With each layer removed, they felt lighter. Clearer. More aligned.

Trusting the Divine Timing

One of the most difficult lessons that the Seeker learned was that the Universe has its own timetable. And that timetable does not tick according to human timetables.

They recalled once when they so wished for something to materialize within a deadline. They thought this was the only way, the only window. But it did not materialize. Not then. Not the way they had envisioned. And it broke their heart.

Yet months later, something far better arrived. Not just a manifestation, but a revelation: had they received their original desire, they wouldn't have been ready. Their soul needed to grow. Their energy needed refinement. Their life needed rearrangement.

What felt like a setback was actually grace disguised as delay.

The Seeker started to live by a new creed: What is mine will come to me. Not when I order it, but when I stand ready to let it come into my open hands and steady heart.

Coming back to Alignment Once Fallen

Every time the Seeker was defeated by life, they had an option: remain bitter or come back to alignment.

It did not involve faking that everything was okay. It involved seeking again and again to trust. To rise up, even when exhausted. To practice meditation, even when skeptical. To speak love, even when wounded.

They learned spiritual resilience—a sort of holy grit. They learned how to float on the emotional waves without being submerged by them. They learned that compassion was stronger than criticism.

They lit candles on nights that seemed dark. They read their own words when their own faith faltered. They reminded themselves who they were becoming—not in spite of the setbacks, but because of them.

And gradually, the light returned. Not a blinding flash, but a warm glow. The lamp of the soul rekindled through commitment.

A New Perspective on the Path

By this time, the Seeker had walked so far that they could turn around and notice a pattern. Each closed door had opened to a better door. Each detour had brought them closer to their authentic self.

They no longer dreaded setbacks. They started embracing them as indications of the soul's growth. As pruning before blossoming. As calibration before alignment.

And they vowed to themselves: I will continue to show up. Even when it gets tough. Especially when it gets tough. Because I know that something holy is going on underneath.

They no longer identified setbacks with failure. They understood them as part of the holy rhythm of life: inhale, exhale. Rise, fall. Create, destroy, recreate.

Embracing the Becoming

Ultimately, the Seeker understood manifestation wasn't about getting—it was about becoming. And becoming was complicated. Nonlinear. Full of tests and triumphs.

The Seeker bore scars now—not of failure, but of expansion. They bore them not with shame, but with pride. Each scar said: I was there. I was tested. I held on. I became.

And so when new seekers arrived at them, tired and bewildered, they didn't provide superficial optimism or easy solutions. They provided presence. They said:

"I know what it is to break apart. I know the pain of waiting. I know the silence of unanswering prayers. But I also know this—nothing is ever wasted. Your tears water the soil. Your pain opens your heart. Your delay deepens your strength.". Keep moving forward. The light you are seeking is already within you. And one day you'll look around and realize—every obstacle was positioning you for something better."

And from that, **the Seeker no longer became simply a manifestor of dreams, but a beacon for others—a soul who recognized the path through the storm and into the sunrise.**

"THE ULTIMATE SECRET TO HAPPINESS"

1. Be grateful for everything you have received in your life (past).

2. Be grateful for everything you are receiving in your life (present).

3. Be grateful for what you want in your life, as though you have received it (future).

-WHY UNIVERSE?

CHAPTER FIVE

YOUR OWN SUCCESS STORY

"Where the Path Ends, the Journey Begins Again"

The sun had fallen below the horizon, and colors of gold and violet had spread across the sky. Silence came over the earth as the Seeker stood in stillness, drinking in the burden and awe of the journey that had just passed. The path had been long. It had wound through valleys of doubt, climbed over peaks of faith, and traversed bridges made of belief. And here they were, not at a conclusion, but at a stunning vista point, at last understanding clearly what was always true.

This tale was never about intentions or manifestations or wishes granted. It was about becoming. About recalling. About remembering the truth embedded in each heart: you are not different from the Universe. You are it—living, breathing, creating.

The Seeker closed their eyes and took a deep breath. Each step, each tumble, each whispered prayer had led them to this. To this knowing. To this clarity. To this moment of quiet that hummed with a sacred invitation:

Now it is your turn.

The Spark Within You

You, the reader, the dreamer, the soul with this book in your hands—you're not merely witnessing another person's tale. You're standing in the prologue of your own victory story. Whatever you read, whatever truths resonated in you, was never about anyone else. It was a reflection. A sign. A whisper.

You've always had the spark. Even in the quiet moments when it felt like the light had gone out, it was there—flickering beneath the surface, waiting for breath, for belief, for boldness.

And now, your soul is stirring again. You've been reminded of your power. Of your potential. Of your divine right to dream and to receive.

But this story won't be written by chance. It will be written by choice.

You Are the Author Now

The Seeker's journey—woven through belief, intention, gratitude, visualization, setbacks, and trust—was never meant to be a prescription. It was a reminder of what is possible when a soul dares to believe.

But your story will be different. It has to be.

Because your heart holds different dreams. Your wounds sing different songs. Your lessons, your strengths, your timing—they are entirely your own.

And this is the magic of manifestation: there is no single way. No flawless formula. No cosmic blueprint.

There is only alignment.

And alignment occurs when your thoughts are aligned with your truth, when your feelings embody your vision, and when your actions respect your soul's path.

Write your story not in fear, but in fire. Not in timidity, but with hunger. Not by aping others, but by moving courageously toward the life only you can build.

Remember Where You Started

Look back for a moment.

You may have started this path feeling unsure, burdened by the world's doubts. You might have wondered if manifestation even existed, if the Universe actually hears, if you were deserving of getting what you truly want.

But see how far you've come.

You now see that manifestation is not simply about daydreaming a car, a house, or a partner. It's about being in the vibration of what you desire. It's about being the you who would magnetically draw to them what they once pursued.

It's about letting go of timelines while maintaining the vibration. It's about having faith in the unseen. About trusting even when there is no evidence.

And most of all, it's about loving more than you fear. More than once.

This is your power now. This is your base. And from here, anything can happen.

Rise Above the Noise

The world will distract you. It will present you with fear in refined guises—cynicism, reason, sameness. It will tell you that dreams are naive, that wonder is make-believe, that the Universe doesn't care.

But now you know the truth.

You've known it in your heart. You've witnessed it in the synchronicities. You've heard it in the silence. The Universe isn't ignoring you—it's within you. It is molding itself by your belief, your words, your vibration.

When things get tough—and they will—know that you are not damaged. You are being refined.

When fears intrude in the darkness, shout your truth. When the world tells you to "be realistic," be miraculous.

And when you are lost, return to this: you are becoming. And becoming is a process that takes time. But you are on the journey. You are on your journey.

Your Manifestation Journal Begins Now

No more waiting for permission.

You are ready to write your tale—not someday, but today.

Begin today.

Light a candle not only in your bedroom, but in your soul.

Write your intentions, not with fearful hope, but with radical faith.

Speak your affirmations as declarations, not wishes.

Meditate not to escape the world, but to remember your place within it.

And walk each day as if the Universe is conspiring for your greatness—because it is.

Be the Mirror

Your journey will not end here. And neither will your impact.

As you emerge, others will observe. They will be inspired not by your flawlessness, but by your tenacity. Not by what you accomplish, but by how you trust.

You will become the mirror that bounces reflection back to the ones who have forgotten their spark.

You will be the embodiment of the fact that everything is possible. That the future is not predicated on the past. That miracles are not for the privileged few, but for anyone who has faith.

You will be living testament to the fact that success is not a destination—it's a frequency.

And your success story will be another's beginning.

And Now. The Ending That Is Not an End

The Seeker once stood where you stand now—at the edge of the unknown, heart ajar, soul prepared.

They made the first move, never knowing where it would take them. And here you are now, standing on holy ground, pen poised, heart pulsating with the still thunder of destiny.

You are no longer reading someone else's tale.

You are writing yours.

With each passing day, you will turn a new page.

With every thought, you will build the next sentence.

With every conviction, you will mold the narrative.

And one day, the tale that was born out of doubt will become a tale of power. The tale that at one point dared to ask "How?" will now declare "I am."

But before the book closes on this chapter, let one more truth resound in the hallways of your heart:

"The Universe has not revealed all its secrets."

"Your greatest manifestation is yet to be revealed."

"And in the stillness between a breath and another, a new book awaits."

"Not inscribed in ink,
but in vibration."

"Not subtitled with clarity,
but with intrigue."

"Not concluded in ending,
but in opening."

An opening...

To go further.

To perceive further.

To become more.

So as you finish reading this book, listen.

Do you hear it?

The call to awaken.

The call to recall.

The call to start anew.

in the next book.

"I SEE THE BIGGER PICTURE. TRUST ME, EVERY MOMENT IS FOR YOUR GROWTH."

-WHY UNIVERSE?

About The Author

NIHAL MUDGAL is an award-winning author, manifestation expert, registered mental health counselor & founder of UNIVERSEA currently pursuing their medical education at Index Medical College, Indore. With a profound dedication to spirituality, self-transformation, healing, and human potential, Nihal has consistently worked to unveil the deep and intricate connections between the universe, consciousness, and the mind.

Nihal Mudgal is the author of the widely acclaimed books **"WHY UNIVERSE?"** and **"HOW UNIVERSE?"**—transformational works that have guided thousands on their journey of understanding manifestation, universal laws, healing, and aligning with cosmic energy. Nihal's distinctive approach harmonizes ancient spiritual wisdom with cutting-edge psychological and scientific insights, empowering readers with practical tools to awaken their true potential.

A lifelong learner and seeker, Nihal holds a Professional Diploma in Clinical Psychology from the renowned University Emo Matrix, and is now an officially registered and practising mental health counselor in India, the United States, and the United Kingdom. This allows Nihal to bring a truly global and interdisciplinary perspective to the fields of healing and mental well-being

Nihal's work continues to inspire individuals across the globe to step into their highest selves, co-create their realities with the universe, and live purposefully. Drawing inspiration from diverse philosophical and spiritual traditions, and integrating insights from neuroscience, quantum physics, psychology, and economics, Nihal helps individuals transform their lives through inner alignment and universal understanding.

Their contributions to the realm of manifestation, emotional healing, and personal evolution have been honored with **The prestigious 2025 Influencer Book of Records Award**. Beyond writing, Nihal is deeply committed to educating and equipping people with the wisdom, clarity, and tools needed to heal, grow, and manifest a life of abundance, impact, and joy.